19.95

GALE FREE LIBRARY
23 Highland Street
Holden MA 01520

Circulation .. 829-0228
Reference .. 829-0229
Children's .. 829-0230

Join the
FRIENDS OF GALE FREE LIBRARY
829-2717

The Play's the Thing

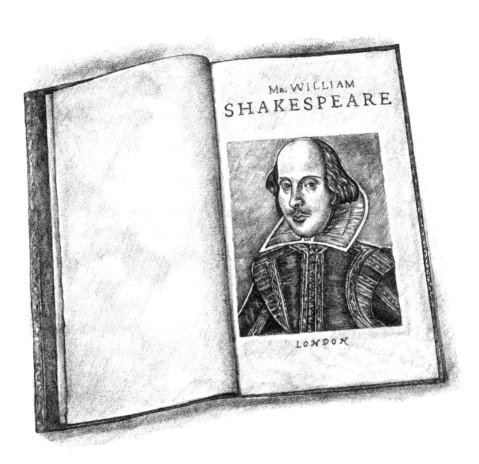

The Play's the Thing

A Story about William Shakespeare

by **Ruth Turk**
illustrations by Lisa Harvey

A Creative Minds Biography

Carolrhoda Books, Inc./Minneapolis

To all my students, wherever they may be, who turned on to William Shakespeare along with their English teacher

Text copyright © 1998 by Ruth Turk
Illustrations copyright © 1998 by Lisa Harvey
Map on page 6 by Laura Westlund, copyright © 1998 by Carolrhoda Books, Inc.

Carolrhoda Books, Inc., c/o The Lerner Publishing Group
241 First Avenue North, Minneapolis, MN 55401 U.S.A.

Website address: www.lernerbooks.com

Library of Congress Cataloging-in-Publication Data

Turk, Ruth.
  The play's the thing : a story about William Shakespeare / by Ruth
Turk ; illustrations by Lisa Harvey.
     p.   cm. — (Carolrhoda creative minds book)
  Includes bibliographical references (p.   ) and index.
  Summary: Traces the life of the famous English writer, from his
childhood and schooling in Stratford-upon-Avon, through his successful
career as actor and playwright in London, to his death in 1616.
  ISBN 1-57505-212-1 (alk. paper)
     1. Shakespeare, William, 1564–1616—Biography—Juvenile literature.
2. Dramatists, English—Early modern, 1500–1700—Biography—
Juvenile literature. [1. Shakespeare, William, 1564–1616. 2. Authors,
English.] I. Harvey, Lisa, ill. II. Title. III. Series.
PR2895.T85   1997
822.3'3—dc21   9710849
[B]

Manufactured in the United States of America
1 2 3 4 5 6 – MA – 03 02 01 00 99 98

Table of Contents

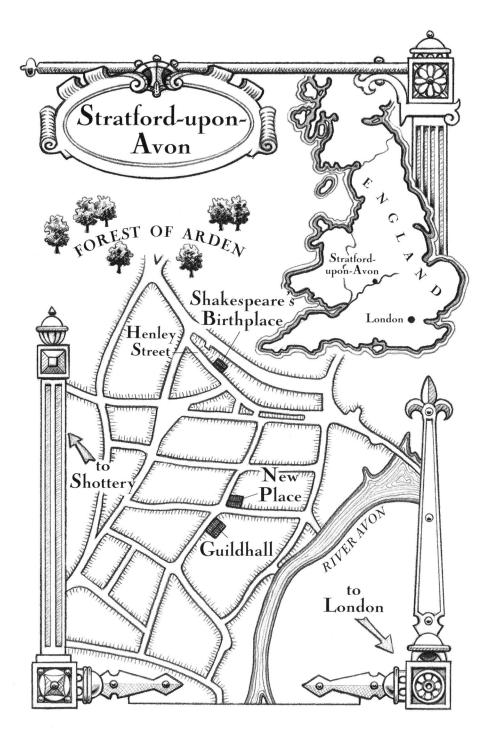

Author's Note

William Shakespeare was born in the 1500s, more than four hundred years ago. He didn't keep a journal, and nobody thought to save his letters or write about his life while he was alive—nobody knew he would one day be considered one of the greatest writers of all time. How, then, can we get to know the man who wrote some of the most enduring lines in the English language?

Researchers have carefully gathered all the documents they could find that had anything to do with the life of William Shakespeare and the people who knew him. There are certificates of baptism, marriage, and burial. There are records of plays performed and property purchased, and there is Shakespeare's will.

Shakespeare also left a legacy of nearly 40 plays and more than 150 poems that tell us about the kind of man he was.

Over the years, many tales have been told about William Shakespeare, some of them true, some of them merely stories. I have tried to separate fact from fiction and put together a meaningful picture of the boy and the man who was William Shakespeare.

I hope that after reading about Shakespeare's life, young readers will experience his plays and poetry for themselves and enjoy his work for many years to come.

1

Stratford-upon-Avon

It was a special day in Stratford-upon-Avon. A company of traveling actors was coming to perform a play. Stratford was about ninety miles west of London. Sometimes the small English town had public fairs with clowns, acrobats, jugglers, and performing animals. But in 1569, a stage production with real, live actors was something most of the townspeople had never seen.

Stratford's mayor, John Shakespeare, had paid the actors out of the town funds, so the show would be free. He knew that if people enjoyed the first performance, they would be willing to pay to attend future shows.

As the news of the exciting event spread, a crowd of curious people gathered in front of the Guildhall, where the performance would take place. Among them was five-year-old William Shakespeare.

10

William watched as the actors and their helpers unloaded the carts and carried their costumes and props inside the hall. They needed to work quickly. If they started the performance too late in the day, they would have to light the hall with candles and torches and risk starting a fire. The actors also knew that the audience could get restless if the play did not begin on time.

The hall's few seats were reserved for town officials. Most of the audience would have to stand in the back. Young William knew he would get to watch from the front row because his father was the mayor. The small boy might have to stand between his father's legs, but he would be able to see everything.

There is no record of what the first play in Stratford-upon-Avon was about. It might have been a comedy with funny characters and music, or a drama with heroes and villains and lots of swordplay, but it was obviously a success, because the actors were invited to return.

The performance gave William and his friends a lot to talk about and even to act out themselves. It wouldn't have mattered that they didn't have the right props or that they didn't remember most of the words of the grand speeches. With a little imagination, a wooden stick could become a sword and a big platter a shield. Many of the boys in Stratford-upon-Avon would grow up to be farmers or shopkeepers, but one of them, William Shakespeare, would become first an actor, then a playwright.

Born on April 24, 1564, William was John and Mary Shakespeare's third child. Two infant daughters had died before William was born, and for a while, the young parents worried that their firstborn son would not live, either. The town had been stricken with a disease known as the plague, and many had died. Fortunately, little William did not get sick and soon grew into an active, normal boy.

The Shakespeare family lived in a house on Henley Street. William and his brothers and sisters were probably born in the room above the living room. When the family grew too large for the house, they bought the house next door. The two houses shared a wall, so it was a simple matter to connect them by putting in a door. One section of the house served as the living quarters, and the rest was John Shakespeare's leather shop. William's father made gloves for the fashionable people of Stratford-upon-Avon. The gloves were made from soft white leather, sometimes richly embroidered or beaded. They were expensive, and only wealthy customers could afford to buy them.

John Shakespeare had not always owned his own leather shop. At one time, he had been a butcher's assistant, but he worked hard, saved his money, and was able to move up in the community. In addition to his mayoral duties, the ambitious glove maker acted as a justice of the peace, trying local law cases and performing marriage ceremonies.

Despite all these activities, Mr. Shakespeare's fondest dream was to become a gentleman and have his own coat of arms. A coat of arms was a symbol that represented a family. These symbols were often very colorful and included figures such as harps, flowers, lions, and sometimes unicorns. A coat of arms was something money alone could not buy. It was an honor granted to people of influence and high standing in the community, and it was passed down to their children. John Shakespeare hoped the honor would soon be granted to him.

As William grew older, he worked in his father's leather shop, helping out as much as possible. Beginning at the age of five, however, he spent most of his time in school. Education played an important part in the life of boys growing up in the town of Stratford-upon-Avon.

2

School Days

From age five to age seven, William went to petty school to prepare for admission to grammar school. At petty school, he practiced saying grace before and after meals. He also learned to write letters and numbers with a goose-quill pen. William wrote in a style known as secretary hand. It wasn't as fancy as the italic style of writing that had recently been popular in England, but it was much faster.

Young William learned how to read from something called a hornbook. A hornbook was a rectangular wood frame with a handle at the end. It looked like a hand mirror. On the flat surface was a page of printed letters covered with a thin, transparent sheet of animal horn. The horn covering protected the paper from dirty fingers, rain, and other damage.

By 1571 William was ready for grammar school. He entered the King's New School in Stratford, which was open to boys only. At that time, people believed girls should learn how to take care of a home instead of going to school. The exceptions were the daughters of wealthy families, who could receive private tutoring if their parents approved.

William got up early every morning, in summer and winter. After washing quickly with cold water, he would carefully dress and comb his hair, because a neat appearance was a strict requirement for an English schoolboy. After saying good-bye to his parents, he collected his books and started out for school. There were thick woods nearby that tempted a young boy to play, but William had to turn toward the center of town. He would walk from his house on Henley Street to Market Cross, then turn right and travel two more blocks to the Guildhall. There he joined his classmates, and together they climbed the stairs to the schoolroom on the second floor. William's classroom was directly above the Stratford council room, where his father met with other town council members once a month.

The school day was long. It started at six in the morning with prayers, which were followed by lessons until nine. During the next half hour, the students had breakfast. Then they resumed their lessons. William went home for lunch at eleven o'clock and returned at one for the afternoon session. School ended at five, after evening prayers. The students had two half days off each week.

During the winter, when not much light crept through the narrow windows of the schoolroom, the students read by candlelight. Every student had to supply his own books, pens, ink, and candles, which he carried to and from school in a small bag.

The school was called grammar school because the students spent most of their time studying Latin grammar. The more advanced students were allowed to learn Greek as well, and they read and memorized long passages of poetry in both Greek and Latin. The students also studied the Bible, but subjects like math and science were not taught. Though his studies were not very exciting, William never forgot what he learned in that classroom in Stratford. When he grew older and started to write plays, he was able to refer to the poetry he had studied years before.

Public speaking was one part of the school program that proved to be especially valuable for William. Reciting from plays by Greek and Roman writers gave him the experience he would need as an actor one day. All that memorizing could have become boring, if not for the interesting meanings of the words and the beautiful sounds they made when they were spoken.

Schoolmasters, as teachers were called, did not think it important to make schoolwork lively or entertaining for their students. School was a place for serious study. Laughter and inattention were punished swiftly and without exception.

Schoolmasters usually administered punishment in three stages. The first time a boy misbehaved, the schoolmaster gave him a stern scolding. If the boy continued in the same way, he had to stay after school and copy endless pages of exercises. The final punishment was the kind few naughty boys challenged more than once. Two or three of the biggest pupils were ordered to hold down the troublemaker while the schoolmaster delivered a number of sharp blows with a thick birch rod. For the next few days, the troublemaker did his schoolwork in the only position he found comfortable—standing up.

When William and his classmates had time off from

school, they played outdoors. They enjoyed fishing, archery, playing ball, and running. In warm weather, they splashed in the cool waters of the River Avon.

Hunting was another popular sport. Hunters snared birds with nets. They shot deer with bows and arrows after tracking them with specially trained hunting dogs. William enjoyed the excitement of the chase, but he did not join his friends in the killing of the animals.

By 1575 John Shakespeare had built a new wing onto his house on Henley Street because his family was still growing. There were now five children. Eleven-year-old William had two younger brothers and two younger sisters, as well as a number of cousins and friends, for playmates. One of William's friends was Richard Field, the son of a neighboring shopkeeper. On their half days off from school, the two boys explored the leafy green Forest of Arden near the town.

When he was sixteen, William graduated from King's New School, knowing that his formal education was at an end. John Shakespeare wanted his son to go on to Oxford University, but the Shakespeares could not afford the great expense. Though Mr. Shakespeare had been quite successful in business up until then, he suddenly began to have trouble. He owed money for back taxes and went deeply into debt.

Soon William's father stopped going to church because he was afraid the sheriff's officers would find him there and arrest him for debt. Though John Shakespeare wasn't the only one who stayed away from church for this reason, it was a painful experience for someone who wished to be held in good standing by the community. It also meant that Mr. Shakespeare's dream of becoming a gentleman with his own coat of arms might never come true.

William pitched in to help his father as much as possible. For the next two years, he learned how to make gloves and sell them to the people of Stratford. William knew that working in a leather shop was a practical occupation for a young man, but it wasn't what he wanted to do with his life.

3

Family Man

By the age of eighteen, William Shakespeare had grown into a pleasant, well-spoken young man. With his family background and grammar school education, he knew the right thing to say at the right time. Some of the young women who came to inspect the lovely gloves and other accessories in the leather shop must have found the glover's son attractive, but William was interested in someone who lived in the next town.

On the long summer evenings, after he was finished with work, William would venture across the meadow into the village of Shottery. There he met Anne Hathaway, the oldest daughter of a well-to-do farmer.

Anne was eight years older than William, but the age difference did not matter to him. On the contrary, he may have found the older woman more interesting because she was so different from the Stratford girls his age.

Anne's father, Richard Hathaway, was eager to see his oldest daughter married, because in those days an unmarried woman of twenty-six was considered almost too old to find a husband. There were also two younger daughters at home who needed to find husbands. A few months later, when Anne told her father that she and William were expecting a child, Mr. Hathaway made swift arrangements for a wedding to take place. On Saturday, December 1, 1582, William Shakespeare and Anne Hathaway were married in a quiet ceremony.

Following the custom of the times, the groom took the bride to live in his parents' home on Henley Street. Though William and Anne had their own living quarters, it was quite crowded, because William's brothers, Richard, Edmund, and Gilbert, and his sister Joan lived in the house as well.

Six months after their marriage and one month after William's nineteenth birthday, William and Anne's daughter Susanna was born. Even for the 1500s, nineteen was a young age to become a husband and father. Two years later, in 1585, Anne gave birth to twins, named Judith and Hamnet. William's income as an assistant in his father's glove shop would not support a wife and three children. He searched for a position as a local schoolmaster and was able to find one in a town near Stratford. Fortunately, he didn't need a university education to teach in a local school.

For the next two years, William taught small boys the same subjects he had been taught as a grammar school pupil. The young schoolmaster realized he didn't want to be a teacher for the rest of his life.

When different acting companies came from London to perform, William didn't miss a performance. He was fascinated by what he saw and heard on the stage, just as he had been when he was a small child. William's love of the theater was growing stronger all the time.

After teaching Latin verbs all day, William tried to write poetry at night. It was nearly impossible to find a quiet spot in the badly crowded house on Henley Street. He became more and more frustrated. William did not have much in common with his former classmates, who were now mostly shopkeepers and farmers, and his friend Richard Field had left for London some time before.

William began to dream of going to London to find

work in the theater. When he told his wife about his dream, she became very upset. But the pressures of his job, his early marriage, and his crowded surroundings finally became too much for William. In 1587 he decided to leave home.

William asked his parents to watch out for his family while he was away and promised to send money for their care. Then he packed a bag and kissed his wife and three children good-bye. With a sword to defend himself against highwaymen, he started down the road to London.

4

On to London

In the late 1500s, London was one of the largest and most exciting cities in Europe. William Shakespeare's hometown of Stratford-upon-Avon, with only two thousand people, could not compare with the busy, crowded metropolis of two hundred thousand. Though London was only ninety miles from Stratford, to the young traveler it was like a city on another planet.

As William wandered through the city streets, he tried to take in the unfamiliar sights on every side. He found London Bridge, a huge structure spanning the River Thames. William had never seen anything like it. All kinds of boats moved constantly back and forth under the bridge's twenty arches, which were supported by sturdy piles of stone. Small boats known as wherries did big business taking passengers up and down the river to their destinations.

On the bridge, William saw tall, narrow apartment buildings joined at the top by a common roof. In the apartments lived tradespeople who sold their wares in the tiny shops below. As he moved along the bridge, William was barely able to squeeze between the many coaches, carts, and horse riders jostling each other as they tried to pass. Not wanting to be struck down by the bumping vehicles, William and the other pedestrians were forced to hug the wall for support.

William gazed in admiration at the row of elegant mansions—homes belonging to royalty and the wealthy—that stood along the banks of the river. If Queen Elizabeth had been expected, all river traffic would have stopped. Sometimes the queen would make a spectacular appearance by torchlight. When she opened the houses of Parliament, she was carried through the streets wearing a red velvet cloak and a gold crown, with twenty-four elaborately dressed maids of honor riding single file behind her.

The Elizabethan period, the years that Queen Elizabeth I ruled England, was a time of great style and exaggeration for the rich. The fashion shows brought excitement to the ordinary lives of those who could only afford to watch.

As William grew more accustomed to the great city, he discovered that the center of fashionable activity was St. Paul's Cathedral. The cathedral was more than just a place of worship. There, Londoners of every social class gathered to gossip, shop, and even conduct business. Strange as it seems, shopkeepers were allowed to set up display stands and sell merchandise inside the cathedral. Paul's Walk, as the middle aisle was called, drew curious sightseers as well as customers. Despite these distractions, there were still prayer services at the front of the cathedral throughout the day.

William had to find a place to live. Since his funds were limited, he looked in the poorer section of the city. In the dark, winding back streets of London, dozens of tenement apartments were squeezed close together, with scarcely any open spaces between them. Children dressed in tattered rags chased each other back and forth over the cobblestones, playing games. They frequently stopped to snatch a crust of bread or anything else they could find to eat in the rubbish. Beggars crawled from the doorways, thrusting out their hands to plead for money or food. It did not matter how sorry William felt for the people in the slums. He had no money to give them, and he knew he couldn't live there.

On the outskirts of the city, William saw a large outdoor amphitheater. In one area, a noisy crowd cheered as they watched a bearbaiting contest. This was a bloody contest in which a bear tied to a stake tried to fight off a pack of dogs. In another area, two bulls were being prodded with sharp sticks so they would attack each other for the amusement of the spectators. People often bet money on which of the poor animals would survive.

In Elizabethan times, both rich and poor people flocked to see the bearbaiting and bullbaiting shows. Public executions were another grisly source of entertainment. Criminals frequently went to their death like actors, delivering speeches to cheering crowds as they stood before the scaffold where they would be hanged.

William had not traveled so far to see such forms of entertainment. At long last, he found a large, circular wooden building with its roof open to the sky. The building was a playhouse called the Theatre. It was the first building in England built especially for plays. (When more playhouses were built, they were called theatres—later *theaters* in American English—after the first playhouse.) A flag flying from the roof signaled that a play would be performed that afternoon. Many people had arrived earlier because they wanted to visit with friends, drink ale, and eat before the performance.

At the sound of a trumpet, people began to crowd toward the entrance. Wealthy people were able to pay extra for a seat in the covered galleries, but William was not one of them. He paid the penny admission and pushed inside with the other "groundlings," who had to stand during the entire show. Standing was not a hardship for someone who loved the theater as much as William did.

No one knows how William Shakespeare got his start in London theater. Some say he got a job moving stage scenery around and prompting players when they missed a line. Others believe that James Burbage, the owner of the Theatre, hired William to hold the horses of wealthy patrons while they watched a performance. The story is told that William was such a courteous attendant and the players were so impressed with the way he spoke, that he soon moved up in the theater.

William was able to find lodging in Shoreditch, a neighborhood not far from the theaters, where many actors lived. The twenty-three-year-old schoolmaster from Stratford was soon immersed in the exciting world of London theater.

5

Actor Turned Playwright

William had a lot to learn if he was going to be a successful actor. He had to be able to handle a sword and duel realistically without causing injuries. He also had to train his voice to reach the top gallery of the theater. It was often necessary for an actor to play a different character each time a play was performed, so William had to memorize many different parts.

There were some parts that William couldn't play. During Elizabethan times women were not permitted to appear onstage, so their roles had to be played by the younger men in the company. Elaborate Elizabethan dresses could be draped to disguise a young man's shape, and the addition of wigs, ruffs around the neck, and other ornaments helped turn male actors into convincing women onstage.

Though William was slender, his general appearance made him look older than his twenty-three years—too old to play the younger or female roles. His hair had started to recede, and his large, sloping forehead made him appear even more mature. William had to find ways to qualify for other parts. When he grew a small goatee (a beard trimmed to a point on his chin) and a mustache, it was easier to portray the role of a king or a nobleman.

William's apprenticeship was quite demanding and didn't earn him much of a salary to send home to his family, but it had certain benefits. It taught him what made a play successful. It also helped him to understand how actors think and feel—something that would come in handy when he wrote his own plays.

As theater became more and more popular in London, many playwrights arrived in the city to try their hand at a writing career. Few people were both actors and writers, but in the early 1590s, William Shakespeare became one of them.

The basic ideas of Shakespeare's plays were not original. It was common for playwrights of the time to look to other works for inspiration. Most of William's ideas came from Greek and Roman writers, but he breathed new life into the characters and gave the old plots new and exciting twists.

William didn't intend his plays to be serious literature. He just wanted them to be entertaining. He wrote comedies to make people laugh, tragedies to make people cry, and histories that told theatergoers the story of their own people.

Shakespeare's plays were full of action. Elizabethan audiences enjoyed watching fierce battles acted out onstage. The shouts of soldiers, the clash of swords and armor, and the roar of a cannon all added to the excitement. For battle scenes, actors would prick containers of sheep's blood carried under their costumes so they would "bleed" realistically. The bloody scenes received appreciative shouts and loud applause from audiences accustomed to the gory spectacle of bearbaiting and bullbaiting.

One of Shakespeare's first works was *Henry VI,* a three-part history play that tells the story of the English king Henry VI and the Wars of the Roses. The play was performed at a theater called the Rose in the spring of 1592 and was a great success.

Theatergoers liked Shakespeare's witty, fast-paced dialogue. *The Comedy of Errors,* one of William's first comedies, kept audiences laughing and guessing how all the plot twists would turn out, until the very last scene. The play is about identical twin brothers, who are both named Antipholus. The twin brothers have identical twin servants, who are both named Dromio. Both sets of twins were separated when they were young children, so they don't know about each other. There are plenty of comical mix-ups before the twins finally meet and everything gets straightened out.

Shakespeare's plays became increasingly popular, and he finally began to make money. But in 1593, London was struck by the plague, the same disease that had killed so many people in Stratford when William was a baby. Thousands of people died. To prevent the spread of the disease, all public meetings and entertainment were banned.

Theaters in London were forced to shut down. People who could afford to leave London moved to the country. The only places those who stayed were permitted to assemble were churches, where they could pray for their loved ones to be spared. Markets, shops, and businesses closed, and people remained indoors as much as possible.

While the theaters were closed, William was able to spend some time in Stratford-upon-Avon with his wife and children. His daughter Susanna was nearly ten years old, while the twins, Judith and Hamnet, were eight. William also used this time to write. He dedicated two long poems to the earl of Southampton.

The poems were called "Venus and Adonis" and "Lucrece." The wealthy nobleman was very pleased and showed his appreciation by giving Shakespeare a generous gift of money, which helped support William and his family until the theaters opened again more than a year later.

6

All the World's a Stage

When the theaters reopened in London in 1594, Shakespeare was a member of an acting company called the Lord Chamberlain's Men. The company was based at James Burbage's playhouse, the Theatre. William was more than just an actor and a playwright for the company. He was also a sharer, which meant he had invested some of his own money in the company and would earn a share of the profits. William Shakespeare's plays made the Lord Chamberlain's Men one of the most popular acting companies in

London, and William's investment in the company made him a wealthy man.

Though William was making a success of his career in London, he hadn't forgotten his family and friends or his hometown of Stratford-upon-Avon. Now that William was well-known and prosperous, he went to work to improve his father's standing in the community. In 1596 the Shakespeares' application for a coat of arms was finally granted. A short time later, William bought New Place, one of the largest houses in Stratford.

These successful years also included a great sorrow for William. In August of 1596, eleven-year-old Hamnet Shakespeare became ill with a high fever and died. William had lost his only son.

As the 1500s were nearing an end, William Shakespeare's plays were becoming more and more popular. He wrote *Romeo and Juliet,* a tragedy about two young people whose battling families wouldn't accept their love. He wrote historical plays such as *Henry IV* and *Julius Caesar.* But during these years, he mostly wrote comedies, with wonderful characters who will never be forgotten.

After joining the Lord Chamberlain's Men, Shakespeare wrote only for his own acting company. This meant he wrote parts with certain performers in mind. Most of his plays included a central role for the company's leading man, Richard Burbage. Richard was the son of James Burbage and a good friend of William's. He was a talented actor known for playing tragic roles. In the early days, he played Romeo in *Romeo and Juliet*. He went on to play the lead roles in Shakespeare's most famous tragedies.

William wrote some of his most humorous characters with comic actor Will Kempe in mind. Kempe, who was a member of the Lord Chamberlain's Men until 1599, was widely known for his lively singing and dancing, and for his unrestrained clowning around onstage. It was no coincidence that Shakespeare wrote some of his best comedies while Kempe was a member of the company.

One of the funniest and best-known roles Shakespeare wrote for Will Kempe was the character of Nick Bottom in *A Midsummer Night's Dream,* a comedy that made fun of romantic love. Much of the play's action takes place in an enchanted forest outside the city of Athens, in Greece. Two young men, Lysander and Demetrius, and two young women, Hermia and Helena, are lost in the forest. Helena loves Demetrius, but both men love Hermia. The king of the fairies, Oberon, orders a mischievous elf named Puck to put magic drops into the eyes of Demetrius so he will fall in love with Helena. But Puck mistakenly gives the drops to Lysander instead of Demetrius. Those same drops make Oberon's queen, Titania, fall in love with a simple weaver named Nick Bottom, the character played by Will Kempe. To add to the fun, the mischievous Puck has given Bottom the head of a donkey, a situation Kempe was able to play with hilarious results.

In 1598 William became involved in one of the most important projects of his life. The lease on the land where the Theatre stood had run out. James Burbage, the man who had built the theater, had died, and the business belonged to his son Cuthbert. The landlord refused to renew the lease unless Cuthbert Burbage agreed to a much higher rent. When Cuthbert complained that the amount was excessive, the landlord declared that he planned to tear down the building. Then he left town.

Under the conditions of the original lease, the tenants of the theater were permitted to take the building apart themselves. When Cuthbert Burbage explained this to the acting company and asked for their help, the group immediately went into action. Putting their money together, the actors and their friends leased a new site on the west bank of the River Thames near London Bridge.

During the night of December 28, 1598, a party of actors and a dozen or more workmen, including a master carpenter, carefully dismantled the theater building, piece by piece. After numbering each section, they stacked the parts in wagons and drove through the wintry streets to the new location. Despite the speed with which they worked, the new theater, which they named the Globe, was completed without mishap.

Like some other early theaters, the Globe was a circular wooden building. It was three stories tall, with its roof open to the sky, and it could hold as many as 2,500 spectators. Clearly visible above the other rooftops, the tall structure was a landmark for miles around. Above the entrance flew a flag showing the Greek god Hercules holding the world, which looked like a globe, on his shoulders.

The first production in the new theater was Shakespeare's comedy *As You Like It*. The play is about a young girl named Rosalind who is banished from the court of her uncle, Duke Frederick. After Rosalind leaves the court, she finds both true love and her father, who is the real duke. In the end, Rosalind's father is restored to his rightful place as duke. As usual, Shakespeare balanced merry laughter with serious comments about life. The second act includes a speech comparing life to a play. These famous lines could be applied to William's own life.

All the world's a stage,
And the men and women merely players:
They have their exits and their entrances;
And one man in his time plays many parts.

William Shakespeare had played many parts in his life, from shopkeeper to teacher to actor. But his most famous role was that of playwright, and at the age of thirty-four, many of his most famous works had yet to be written.

7

For All Time

William Shakespeare's life could easily have ended in 1601. Without realizing what was happening, William and the other members of his acting company became involved in a plot to overthrow the queen.

Among Queen Elizabeth's favorites at court was the earl of Essex, a handsome young nobleman. Despite their relationship, the queen refused to give the earl the power he craved. In 1601 the earl decided to stir up a rebellion to overthrow the queen. The earl of Southampton, who had known Shakespeare for years, agreed to join Essex.

A few days before the planned uprising, some of Essex's friends appeared at the Globe Theatre and offered the Lord Chamberlain's Men a large sum of money to give a special performance of *Richard II,* one of Shakespeare's early plays. In this play an unfit king, Richard, is forced to surrender his throne to a nobleman named Bolingbroke. Essex had the idea that the crowds who saw this play would imagine him as a kind of Bolingbroke and join him in the takeover he was planning. The actors, who didn't know about the earl's plans, accepted the mysterious offer and performed the play.

Despite the performance, when Essex rode through the streets of London trying to rouse followers, people shut their doors against him to show their loyalty to the queen. Essex was arrested and sentenced to death. Though Southampton was allowed to live, he was imprisoned in the Tower of London. The queen questioned the unfortunate acting company. Plotting against the queen was a very serious charge that could cost them their lives. In the end, however, she decided the actors were innocent, and they weren't punished.

That same difficult year, William's father died. William turned away from writing romantic comedies and began to write about more serious subjects. Some of these tragedies concerned great men whose characters weren't strong enough to overcome evil forces. In two of Shakespeare's plays, *King Lear* and *Othello,* the leading characters destroy others and themselves because of their own weakness—much as the earl of Essex had.

One of Shakespeare's most famous tragedies, and perhaps his greatest play, was *Hamlet.* The main character's name was very similar to that of William's son, Hamnet, who would have been nearly grown if he had lived.

Hamlet is the story of a young Danish prince who believes his uncle killed the king—Hamlet's father—in order to marry the queen—Hamlet's mother—and become king himself. The play has many of the acting devices that Elizabethan audiences expected, including asides and soliloquies. In an aside, a character speaks a thought aloud without the other characters onstage hearing it. In a soliloquy, a character standing alone on the stage talks directly to the audience about his or her feelings. In one of Hamlet's soliloquies, the prince wonders whether it is better to live or die when life becomes troubled. The speech, which begins, "To be or not to be," is probably the most quoted soliloquy in English drama.

In 1603 Queen Elizabeth died and the king of

Scotland became the king of England. The new king, James I, happened to be extremely fond of plays. Of all the acting companies in London, his favorite was the Lord Chamberlain's Men, William's company. It wasn't long before the king became the company's patron, which meant he gave them gifts and money and made sure they were treated well. The Lord Chamberlain's Men became known as the King's Men. They were frequent visitors at the palace, and Shakespeare's plays were performed for the king again and again.

Wanting to please the Scottish king, Shakespeare used Scottish history to write *Macbeth,* one of his most dramatic plays. The play, which is full of ghosts and witches and bloody murders, is a fascinating story about a man whose conscience is destroyed by the ambition he can't control.

Macbeth, a brave soldier and nobleman, is over-come with wild ambition when three witches tell him that one day he will be king. Believing the prophecy, he changes from a fine, upstanding person into one who will stop at nothing, not even murder, to get what he wants. Encouraged by his wife, Macbeth murders the king and seizes the throne of Scotland. Macbeth becomes so hardened to killing that he goes on to murder others who stand in his way. In the end,

Macbeth is killed in battle and the son of the murdered king becomes king in his place.

As William entered his forties, he continued to write, averaging about a play a year. Altogether, he wrote nearly forty plays in his lifetime. He also wrote more than a hundred fourteen-line poems called sonnets. Shakespeare's sonnets contain some of the most memorable and beautiful lines in the English language, including "Shall I compare thee to a summer's day?" and "Love is not love which alters when it alteration finds." A book of Shakespeare's sonnets was published in 1609.

No matter what he was writing, Shakespeare constantly found new and colorful ways to express himself. Words like *excellent, majestic, gloomy, leapfrog, lovely, hint, hurry, reliance,* and *bump* were originated by William Shakespeare. Many phrases still used in conversation come from Shakespeare's writing, including "fair play," "dead as a doornail," "budge an inch," "set your teeth on edge," and "own flesh and blood."

In July 1613, Shakespeare's play *Henry VIII* opened at the Globe. As King Henry made his grand entrance, a prop man at the back of the stage fired a cannon. A flying spark landed on the theater's thatched roof and the building burst into flames.

As the crowd rushed to escape, the actors quickly gathered all the costumes and props they could carry from the burning structure. The theater burned to the ground, but no one was killed and Shakespeare's scripts were saved. By the following spring, the theater had been rebuilt, this time with a tile roof.

The King's Men were more successful than ever, but William was ready for a quieter life. He had spent nearly thirty years in London, but Stratford was still home. As he neared fifty, he began to spend most of his time in the comfortable surroundings of New Place, the home in Stratford he had bought years earlier. New Place consisted of a large brick and timber house with a cottage for guests. Surrounded by beautiful gardens, the house was quite a contrast to the bustling crowds and traffic of London.

For the first time, the busy playwright had the leisure to enjoy his family and friends. While he missed his son, Hamnet, William took pleasure in visiting with his now married daughters, Susanna and Judith, and especially his little granddaughter, Elizabeth. From time to time, Stratford friends would drop by to spend the evening talking about old times, as would a few actor friends from London.

In the spring of 1616, William knew something was wrong. He hadn't been feeling well for a few weeks and had come down with a fever. In March he decided to make some adjustments in his will. In spite of his illness, William was as clear about putting his thoughts down in writing as he had always been.

After providing for the members of his family, William left money for the poor people of Stratford. To Richard Burbage, John Heminges, and Henry Condell, three fellow actors who had been close friends, William left money to buy memorial rings, which people wore to remember a friend who had died.

On April 23, 1616, William Shakespeare died. Two days later, he was buried in the Stratford church where he had been baptized fifty-two years earlier. His daughter Susanna had a large marble monument erected on the north wall of the church. The monument was a bust of William Shakespeare placed between two marble columns.

Shakespeare's friends John Heminges and Henry Condell thought so much of William that they wanted to dedicate their own monument to him. They collected William's plays and, seven years after his death, had them published at their own expense in a volume called the First Folio. If not for these two devoted friends, many of Shakespeare's plays might have been lost.

Though Shakespeare's work was popular when he was alive, his reputation has grown far greater since his death. Whether read from a book or performed onstage, his words still have the power to hold people spellbound, four centuries after they were written. William Shakespeare, the son of a Stratford shopkeeper, never dreamed that one day the world would claim him as the greatest playwright that ever lived.

Ben Jonson, a well-known English writer, summed up Shakespeare's genius in the preface to the First Folio when he said, "He was not of an age, but for all time!"

The Plays of William Shakespeare

Comedies
All's Well That Ends Well
As You Like It
The Comedy of Errors
Love's Labour's Lost
Measure for Measure
The Merchant of Venice
The Merry Wives of Windsor
A Midsummer Night's Dream
Much Ado About Nothing
The Taming of the Shrew
Twelfth Night
The Two Gentlemen of Verona

Histories
Henry IV, Parts I and II
Henry V
Henry VI, Parts I, II, and III
Henry VIII
King John
Richard II
Richard III

Romances

Cymbeline
Pericles
The Tempest
The Winter's Tale

Tragedies

Antony and Cleopatra
Coriolanus
Hamlet
Julius Caesar
King Lear
Macbeth
Othello
Romeo and Juliet
Timon of Athens
Titus Andronicus
Troilus and Cressida

There is no record of the exact year in which each play was written. William Shakespeare also wrote more than 150 poems, including his famous sonnets.

Bibliography

Brown, John Russell. *Shakespeare and His Theatre.* New York: Lothrop, Lee & Shepard, 1982.

Chute, Marchette. *An Introduction to Shakespeare.* New York: E. P. Dutton & Co., 1951.

Evans, Garth Lloyd, and Barbara Lloyd Evans. *The Shakespeare Companion.* New York: Charles Scribners Sons, 1978.

Fraser, Russell. *Young Shakespeare.* New York: Columbia University Press, 1988.

Hodges, C. Walter. *Shakespeare's Theatre.* New York: Coward-McCann, Inc., 1964.

Humes, James C. *Citizen Shakespeare.* Westport, Conn.: Praeger Publishers, 1993.

Kay, Dennis. *Shakespeare: His Life, Work, and Era.* New York: William Morrow & Co., 1992.

Lyon, Sue. *Shakespeare's England.* New York: Marshall Cavendish, 1989.

McMurty, Jo. *Understanding Shakespeare's England.* Hamden, Conn.: Archon Books, 1989.

Pearson, Hasketh. *A Life of Shakespeare.* London: Hamish Hamilton Ltd., 1987.

Ross, Steward. *How It Was: Elizabethan Life.* London: B T Batsford Ltd., 1991.

Rowse, A. L. *Shakespeare the Man.* New York: Harper & Row, 1973.

Singman, Jeffrey L. *Daily Life in Elizabethan England.* Westport, Conn.: Greenwood Press, 1995.

Wagenknecht, Edward. *The Personality of Shakespeare.* Norman, Okla.: University of Oklahoma Press, 1972.

Index

About the Author

Ruth Turk started writing at the age of nine and has never stopped. She was an English teacher in the New York school system, where she tried to bring her love of words to children from kindergarten through high school. She has written many books for both young people and adults, including biographies of Ray Charles and Lillian Hellman. Ruth and her educator husband, Len, spend winters in Lake Worth, Florida, and summers in Ithaca, New York.

About the Illustrator

Lisa Harvey is a fifth-generation Montanan. She lives in Helena, Montana, with her husband and two children. Harvey has a B.A. in art from Montana State University and was an art teacher before becoming an illustrator and calligrapher. She enjoys history and has illustrated several books about past events.